MISREPRESENTATION: REPRESENTATION WITHOUT IDENTITY

J. D. STEWART

ISBN-13:9781724207364
ISBN-10:1724207369

"An individual in a crowd is a grain of sand amid other grains of sand, which the wind stirs up at will".

Gustave Le Bon

Table of Contents

Chapter 1

Government

The prospects for a new country hinged on representation over two centuries ago. Taxation without a hand in the governmental game was unacceptable. As a country our forefathers longed for and were willing to die for a free America. To be represented as a free entity was the goal and no one willing to fight for freedom from English tyranny would settle for less. We were to represent our country free and clear of English control, and we still hold our freedom as one of our highest blessings for this United States of America.

Through two world wars and military skirmishes that seem to be unending, American's have participated in the world as leaders in the protection of oppressed people everywhere. With money, military weapons and our physical presents in needy countries, we stand for civil self-representation around the world.

Representation has run to ground in America, however, as Congressional survey's indicate that legislators are not thought to be effective and representative of the needs of the citizenry. The legislatures seem to continually get it wrong.

My wife taught in public school for thirty years. A group of elementary teachers took it upon themselves to ask for planning time like high school teachers have always had. They wanted to be able to send teacher's aides to lunch with the students and spend the time preparing their lessons. Eventually the legislators gave the elementary teachers their wish, but what was passed was not representative of what the teachers had in mind.

In case of a student's birthday, the teacher would like to celebrate at lunch with the class, but the legal ruling that was passed to answer teacher needs specified that teachers could not for any reason sit with their students during lunch. The aides' duties had been modified to take in lunch, so teachers were not allowed to attend since such attention would be thought to be unneeded, or that the aides would be unnecessarily paid for if the teacher were there, not to mention the unspecified authority of the party responsible for looking out for the safety of the students and being paid for that. Money and limited authority are almost always misrepresenting factors in governmental decisions.

But it wasn't just the freeing up of time for teachers to plan lessons. The teachers were bound by law not to sit with their classes. Representation was turned into repression of teacher freedom.

They were given what they wanted and at the same time freedom was taken away. This seemed a correct way to treat the teachers, aides and students since they were not meant to be given extra freedom. Allowing teachers to work on lessons or attend a birthday celebration for their students would have seemed to have been a free perk for contract workers who had not negotiated such a provision in the contract. Give with one hand and take way with the other.

The problem here is too much representation and as a result no representation. The teachers and the union agreed to a compromise with the education department wanting a deal that maintained clear authority of the aides in lunchroom activities for which they would be paid and thus required to be the *in loco parentis* in attendance for a specific legal guarantee for custodial responsibility for aides in the lunchroom. The government lawyers were not going to take a soft position of either teacher or aide being in the lunchroom with the class. It had to be specified which responsible party would be there in case of a legal problem. Someone had to take the fall for accidents or negligence in the lunchroom.

A stipend brought me to public education. Two months in class and nine months at night and I was a teacher of record in my high school classes. The third year of my apprenticeship I was given an extra planning period to help a student that was in the same teacher program in which I had been fast-tracked. Every day I used my extra class period, sat in on this young teacher and passed on suggestions when we could find the time.

Even though I was seeing progress for my efforts, it got around that I had a "free class period" and their was some negative feedback among the faculty. It seem many believed that was not contributing to the common purpose of educating our students. There were many teachers who thought that I was getting out of contract work. These teachers felt that I was not representing them because I had one less class to teach, and I was getting special treatment. There were administrators and coaches that were given light teaching loads but it was expected of them to be given extra time.

As it turned out the young lady became a valued teacher and even moved up to an administrative office toward the end of her tenure. So, why was I labeled a slacker, when it would seem that my work with the teacher had been profitable? In this case teaching was singular. Teacher's come to believe the lie that we are and should all be the same in our teaching responsibilities. I had violated the unspoken rule that we all held the same authority and the same responsibilities. My mentoring during a free period negotiated and paid for by the stipend provider made me look like I was stepping out of my standard role as a teacher and was launching an attempt to become an administrator, for more money and a looser schedule. In this case I did not represent the rank and file, but there have been historic cases after cases where administrative representation has failed to adequately represent the membership effectively.

When the unions had there heyday many workers joined with talk of higher wages and perks ranging from medical to vacation time. Today the unions have lost much of their appeal. Unions do not seem as effective as they once were and memberships are very low. One of the problems that they are having has to do with political leaning: the left is almost always supported by the union leadership while the membership itself tends to vote much more conservatively. This is clear misrepresentation and union dues, in part, are paying for liberal candidates who often do little to improve wages and perks despite their promissory rhetoric.

Allegiance to a political party often results in misrepresentation. Democrats promise the lower class supporters more money but during Obama era there were many new food stamp users. Republicans fight over the particulars of a value bill and usually sacrifice progress to infighting.

When a Republican president takes on the bureaucracy it becomes clear that the bureaucracy does not wish to have its Swamp drained.

So, representatives that we elect want the rule of law to become their tool for themselves only. It doesn't seem too be just Democrats that are obstructionists but many Republicans also. Passing laws should be keeping that which is non-negotiable and compromising on the details. Remember the story of the student lunch prohibition? All issues are seemingly non-negotiable to modern legislatures. For they are afraid that their constituents will vote them out of office if they bend even on the small details of legislation.

Congress has an approval rating in the mid-teens. President Trump is moving up toward 50 per cent. Do we feel like we are represented properly by our congress? It doesn't seem like the presidents policies are finding passage in a Republican congress. Republican cannot agree on the details of any potential bill, and Democrats will not let any thing pass due the requirement of 60 votes for most bills. A few Democrats are needed. The mandate for the president's policies is clear, but Democrats will not hear of it and plan to defeat as many bills as possible. Even immigration which is in the Democrat's best interest - more immigrants, more potential Democratic voters - is being opposed to provide a mid-term issue of blaming lack of immigration laws on the Republicans.

How is this representation? If there is no instant recall of all elected governmental representatives why do we assume that they will represent us on the matters we elected them to address. In the day of computerized life, when an elected official passes the 50% point of failure in his job approval, we should be able to bring them home and elect someone who would do the job properly.

The only reasonable recourse today to such failed representation is term limits. It would either support lower levels of graft, or make them work harder, faster and less carefully in their lawless activities giving authorities a change to catch them. Perhaps a question session with a lie detector or a bonding process where anti policy actions would be tantamount to impeachment, fining and recall.

This would not work for elected officials who do not care about this country but rather lining their pockets with taxpayer and lobbyist graft. It is hard to think that people who run for office care little for Americans and fighting for beneficial legislation for us. How can open boarders to the south help Americans when terrorists and drug smuggling are rampant? Yet Democrats refuse to help seal the southern border with a wall. For the Democrats it means never having to see another Republican administration with illegals soon to gain voting rights and supplement the pool of dead voters in Democratic states.

Perhaps elected "servants" of the people should have to first serve their country in the services where most come to know a reasonable way of viewing our countries needs. Calls for abolishing ICE are merely from those who would see a country of strangers unable to communicate needs and preferences for their lives and obtain ing them illegally and on their own, rather than a vibrate and multicultural melting pot where everyone is respected and generally good wishes are communicated among people of varieties of skin color and english accents. Until we can see these characteristic in American citizens across the board then we will not be able to call America democratic nor "Great."

America is not always in compliance with law. I have written that if you drive down the expressways or freeways doing the speed limit you will be passed by everyone. We do not respect the law that is able to save our lives everyday. This law does not represent us because it is disobeyed by most drivers everyday. There are ways to stop this, but elected officials are not willing to arm cars with speed detection that can be read by police. It might be very efficient if a record of all speeding episodes would be ticketed. Imagine getting multiple tickets when you are stopped. When buying a car the speeding events would be transferred to the new vehicle. Lets say that being ticketed for $100 is now a ticket for 10 offenses or $1000. Would this get our attention?

The call to an uncivil society is the nudging of anarchy by a vocal cacophony in an attempt to magically bring about totalitarianism. The call to disband ICE is a call for chaos, open borders and rule of the strong. The United States could not survive under a flag of mere power but needs a Constitution to hold back the usurpation of despots and a soft government. The Constitution is being interpreted not from law but by personal preference. At this rate there will be no law to protect and guide us.

This issue and others do seem to be registering with millennials as they are beginning to move from Democrat candidates to more mainstream Republican candidates. The misrepresentation of the Democrats and many Republicans requires a closer look at policies and attempt to reconnect supporters to solid policies.

This book is essentially anecdotal in proving the thesis that we are disarming our beliefs by joining groups that do not, and in all honesty, cannot totally represent us in our personal essentialism but will only vocalize a good approximation at best.

Chapter 2

Organizational Evolution

So, if the examples just cited are failures in representation, then how should the process properly work? How can we find reliable representation? The answer is that we cannot, and we must remain alert to the possibilities of change in our membership, issues of detailed policy and drift in principles. Keeping one's ear to the ground can prevent disasters. Know that you can stop these disasters but you must decide if you are willing to get the organizational direction reset when needed or otherwise you must walk away. It should not be your realization that you have changed in attitude. You must change group tenets. If you have changed, then you must sort out reasons and inclinations that have brought you to this new view of the group and more importantly the changes through which you have personally navigated.

In several of my previous writings, a foundational understanding of who we are at the core and how we arrive at that belief point was discussed. A person that has strong beliefs and has justifiable argumentation for embracing a consistent life-guiding internality must defend the core essentialism of day-to-day life and decisions. These core values must be ongoing and consistent. These values are continuously challenged by existential challenges which can be consistently defeated by strong beliefs. On rare occasions experiential input successfully replaces essential ideas, but this is rare for someone who has consistent values which are in agreement and not conflicted. If experience successfully counters essential values, then, if the new values added to one's essential core are in conflict with those values still in place, conflict may leave the inner essential core in confusion and chaos.

Taking on conflicting group purposes or personal purposes and understandings has the same effect, confusion and chaos.

On a founding board of directorship on which I served for a year, the goals were laid out plainly and clearly, but, by the second year, those that were seeking to be appointed in the new directorship had different ideas. They wanted to convert the organization to something different. The founders had no goal to become a major factor in our field. We were, in originary thought, to become an alternative to what was being offered. Those that got into the board in subsequent years saw a different purpose, which required more cash flow. I noticed that the people I would have wanted to see brought into management were not very willing to give their established professional currency to our project. We were relatively unimportant. Those who had little to offer wanted a place on the board to help promote themselves. Within a few years, every activity with which the organization was involved was very high profile, unlike the intended first purpose for which some of us were dedicated.

On the only other non-profit organization board on which I served, very similar results were seen. In this case there were only three of us that founded the organization. Within the first year, I left the group. One of the goals that the other two people on the board held was that the organization would eventually be given over to others. My position was that the community would destroy the original purpose of the project. I left, the community moved in and over time ran my two friends away. They changed the purpose and created a large cash flow problem that required the raising of yearly funds. I was an expendable member of the board, but my two friends who stayed on until they were threatened with prosecution, were the backbone and lifeblood of the project. The new leadership came in below, rose up in the organization, took over, threatened legal action and finally changed the organization to maximize visibility and new interests.

I grew up in a neighborhood Methodist Church. Orthodoxy varied with the pastors that were cycled in and out of the church, as is the Methodist way. The progression seen over my early years of church-going in replacing bastions of belief, was swift and unrelenting. One only has to ask has the Gospel changed in two thousand years? No, Methodism has changed? The president of a large Methodist university was ask if the school was still Methodist in modern times. The response was that, "We are not Christian, but we are still Methodists." As the ideals of Methodism change over time they are at least still Methodist. What does this babbling mean? The Westley's would rollover in their graves to hear of such. The church has left its millennial-old tenets for a better fit with today's church goer. The change overall was relatively slow, with some less theologically minded members being swept along with the evolution, left to intone a new Psalm.

I find myself today being denied the Apple computer's intuitive methodology for learning computer process. Apple kept its own way of doing computer work for almost two decades and then became more PC like with the exception of terminology which did not match with PC terminology and proceeded to obscure any recognition of process. For instance the tern Wi Fi is rarely used compared to PC language and clouds the way that once was clear for Apple owners. Wi Fi may be used in a restaurant without knowing much computer jargon but try to add a devise to your "extended" Wi Fi or bluetooth devises ... now i have once again confused myself. The point is that Apple left me a dozen years ago after I had invested time and energy in understanding a different and intuitive process.

CHAPTER 3

COMMUNITY

M. Scott Peck was a psychiatrist who made a study of individuals within the community. He worked with groups who had aspirations to form community. Peck pointed out two very important tenets of community building: work at community at all times is required, but still there should not be expectations that the community will last forever. A group that has the same demographic or actually lives together within the same community does not necessarily a community make. Community is formed by willing members supporting a group purpose without sacrificing individual identity unless it be absolutely required to be a short term yet important community need. With out the maintenance of individualism within the community the tug and pull of policy issues does not occur, and community cannot survive. You must ask yourself at which moment remain in the community is deleterious too you personal identity.

I have seen many families who could not even under the bond of blood maintain familial communities. This may not seem so surprising since to form a strong family bond personal identity may need to be deemphasized. It is possible that similar identities in families may result in a battle for bio-familial leadership or even breeding rights. The fight for leadership may become highly competitive in tight groups. Power struggles within a family may give rise to feuds and separation. Trying to gain control of the group or family is the first sign of a faulty start. Only strong leadership can take down community efforts. All members of any group must yield to the group effort and not just in lip service but in reality. Failure to find commonality in membership destroys fellowships within families and in focus groups. The goal is to maintain personal identity while giving undying allegiance to the group. In a topical book that I wrote on John Dewey was the measure of the salient philosopher of the twentieth-century America. John Dewey in his long educational career influenced the thinking of millions of teachers and administrators as did his numerous acolytes. The problem inherent in giving individuals authority while expecting group purpose is discussed in my book. In fact the duality of these two goals leaves an inoperable dichotomy which Dewey never could resolve. Dewey believed that radical individuals would come back to their groups in time, a very simplistic understanding of individualism and group membership. Dewey's ideas is the philosophical wave that has settled in America, a pragmatism known as instrumentalism, which only supports purposes active in proof of their proposition. He might say, without the effect of the cause there is only a dream. Although not so academically provoked nor so individually accomplished, most Americans are undoubtedly pragmatic, whatever seems to works. This understanding of individual philosophy among the group membership does not bode well for a strong communitarianism.

John Kerry's run for the Whitehouse in 2004 was plague by an inability to see commonly held issues among all the left-wing individualistic cry-babies. It was reported that he could not find a single theme that would bring him majority support. What we see in general communitarian issues is a strong almost indefatigable sense of mono-focused determination. Gaining one's single most important issue addressed as a consequence of voting for a particular candidate may not be so easy when the diversity of issues may bring conflicts among those holding different positions. There may be issues that please some voters, but some issues may turn off other voters.

Modern individualism is the enemy of sound, purposeful community. We have no answer today for the will of the One. Take for example again the community of expressway cars. The anonymity of people crouched in speeding cars some enclosed in dark wrap-around windows. All are subject to the same rules of the road. No speeding, no passing on the shoulders, these are rules for all to follow.

Yesterday I was in the fast lane (inside lane) because I was going to turn off the expressway from that lane in a mile or so, but the driver behind me was honking for me to get out of the way so she could speed. She finally pulled into an adjacent lane and gave me a dirty look. She wanted me to break the rule on speed in order to allow her to speed. She was threatening me and she passed me. I was being bullied to speed against my will. When is the idea that if all do the right thing and keep all the rules we will all meet our same goal, arriving alive. We all have the same purpose although we have different destinations. We hide in our automotive tin cans disregard the rules set for all drivers alike to be safe, and expecting everyone to accommodate our flirtation with illegality. Most times when I am obeying the road rules, everyone is pulling away from me and those behind me are closing in fast. We, without thinking speed, misrepresent our right to travel free and not to encumber our personal license. If everyone saw their road warrior demeanor, then the roads would consist of mobs of drivers thinking only about themselves.

Chapter 4

Issues of Incongruity

It is time to become a little more analytical as well as anecdotal in examining misrepresentation. I have given the name *incongruity aspect* to describe the insightful perspective of critics of belonging. To have a deep insight into multiple organizational failures is to display *global incongruity aspect*. Incongruity aspect in its global form would not be a recommended position, but would accurately reflect one's imperfection alone and in groups in both profitable as well as charitable groupings. A global individual might spend most of the time alone and alienated. Since there is usually no way to appropriately respond to failures and falsification, globals may never see restitution for abuse, but they will only continue to see the problems in shadows.

Although a group may have a well-known mission statement, it will neglect honoring such core intentions when the group is threatened. Groups claim equality of membership in dealing in emergencies as well as every day functioning. I remember when the twin tower tragedy occurred and the directive by ground zero leaders was to fund the rescue efforts by giving donations to the Red Cross. It was soon recognized that the money given to help its victims, over 500 million dollars, that only 60 % of that money was used on those trapped in the rubble the remainder was set aside for other emergencies. The Red Cross is the trusted organization to which we as kids of the nineteen fifties donated pencils, erasers for European, post World War II children. The Red Cross had reached in its confiscation of funds for organization building due to its *limits of procedure,* that is to consider the good of the organization over integrity, the limits to which it was willing to profit its own survival over service. In the same vein, several years ago SPCA international was using much of its donation money to help fundraising efforts for the organization. They were tasked with saving animals from harm. They like the Red Cross, despite its mission statement, had unwritten *rules of (dis)engagement,* such as preserving the organization at all costs.

When one company is bought out by another the *rules of engagement* are usually altered affecting most of the employees of both companies adversely. The effects can be devastating to both companies as even new territory is scouted out relieving the company of past guarantees of employees' benefits. Medical care, life insurance and retirement packages can evaporate. Certainly an unplanned incongruity could be the denial of a family of an employee lost protection as workers had looked after the business for years, giving in some cases their lives in its defense.

The unwritten rule was to preserve the company and its assets at all cost. even the breaking of promises made to employees.

Chapter 5

Hierarchy

One of the problems with organization is found in hierarchy, or levels of leadership and memberships. The gap between elite and common memberships often covered up by what could be called the *participation trophy generation* or *the ubiquity factor.* Every member is given the same trophy, despite the fact that there were winners and losers.

Hans Selye, a Hungarian endocrinologist, early in the last century discovered how stress affected the body. The body that he studied was that of the rat, but it also applied to all animals and people. He recognized that the lower level rats had much bigger adrenal glands than the leader rats. The so-called stress endocrine organ, the adrenal gland, grew to great size in the lower eschelon rats because they were stressed at the bottom of their social rat cage as they literally crawled all over one another. Selye called his theory General Adaptive Syndrome (GAS) and held that the adrenal gland reacts to any sort of stress (general) and has adverse reactions in the adrenal glands leading to injury or in extreme cases even death. It is an adaptive process in that the body registers the injury to stress and the effects, even if not lethal, are permanent.

All organizations are hierarchical and under the right circumstances can bring on stress and adaptive behavior. For example the history of unions is a good example of stress causing organizations. After the war in the middle of the last century, workers were trying to gain and enjoy the American dream by holding a well paying job with perks like medical care and retirement. The promise of such worker success was the union. Unions defied bosses and management, picketed and even brought in enforcers who were to bring resistance to company policy by aggression and violence. Union organizers not only threatened scabs who would do the work of union employees during strikes but also rioted and all at the expense of the union worker.

Just imagine being a striking worker unable to live comfortably on your wages, but instead received union money, not enough to live well but a payment you could not refuse. The worker on the picket lines was also a victim, stressed by the often illegal and violent roles that were made to play. The union leadership knew their *limits of engagement* even if the rank and file were kept out of the information loop while engaged in even illegal activities prohibited by the courts. Under paid, not knowing if there would be a job at the end of the strike, the worker could not go against the union without getting some of the violent behavior directed toward him. The damaging effects of getting a new contract every few years was a constant aggravation to the workers body, if not in going through the striking process, then expecting it at any time contract or no.

So how common would this general reaction be to stress? A simple example would be the defiant son who awaits his father's return home from the office to receive a spanking as his mother had prepared the boy's mind with stressful threats. The boys has only to wait and ponder his fate, if not a spanking, then loss of child privileges, any form of stress which will leave a life-long biological if not mental scar.

Although we have committed as a culture to carrying out child punishment, we have placed restrictions on physical punishment only to apply stress without physical options. The "spoiling of the child" may be no more damaging than the "rod" or the loss of privilege for punishment. We are in need of punishing children for rebellion or transgressions of many varieties, or otherwise we are to live in a criminal culture where "no" is not wielded with the result that children are corrected. Stressing is the only way to redirect harmful activity. We are the necessary stressors of our children to make them ultimately better citizens, stressed to kindness and love.

Think about dragging yourself off to work each day, when you are sick and preoccupied with family problems the venture may seem torturous. Those at the top of the organization you work for are better paid and have options to take off from work when they wish, and what about the perks, unheard of by the basic worker. The differential in pay along divides and isolates workers from management.

Chapter 6

The Enlightenment

The Enlightenment Project, begun as early as the beginning years of the seventeen century, changed the way that the individual was to see self. In fact enlightenment, although dedicated to reason, was to turn the individual out into the world with a drive to know. Metaphysical mysteries were jettisoned, and, since reason could not be applied, love and hate, religion and charity were seen as un-reasonable with, therefore, no way to truly know them. This monolithic knowing was to propel the individual to heights of intractable disregard for others and community. It marked the beginning of communal tolerance and a shelving of a broad and unified workable belief system.

There was a sense that individual difference before the enlightenment project was a crude yet necessary affectation of belonging. Differences were no celebrated but accepted as meaning individuality, not based on the closed-mindedness of cerebral ascension to truth. In fact we have lost a broader understanding of truth. To be true to an ideal or another person was valued as truth in action.

The rise of the unfettered individual has caused a widening gulf among persons and community members. The Project was tapped to have a dependable way to know factually with the scientific method to guide inquiry into fact finding. Religion and metaphysics in general were left alone initially with necessity answering a spiritual call. If God were needed for an argument, then he would be taken out and made available for *deus ex machina* in the denouement. When God and the metaphysical scaffolding of the world was neglected, then the distance between individuals was broadened.

The enlightenment left individuals separated with reason being the prime if not the only question. God if referred to at all was to be reasoned and proved, the necessity. Reasoned communities looked only to thought. This was institutionalized in The Royal Academy (of Science) which from the mid-sixteen hundreds held the standards for scientific reasoning and largely influenced by Sir Francis Bacon with his book, *New Atlantis.* In the book Solomon's House was seen as a place for discovery, a place to do research and influence the scientific and provide a healthful future of man. One of its main functions was to pass on acceptable knowledge, that is actually the sanctioned understandings of the Academy. The Enlightenment promised thought with a challenge to accepting ideas and facts that are proven and soundly reasoned. In its early history alchemy was overcome by science. Isaac Newton, an early member of the Academy, did not know whether science would win out over alchemy, and his dominant interest in religion in his later years was not favored by the membership.

All of this is to say that there was much mind control in the Academy, the scientific constraints of the scientist. There were ways of study, and, without conforming to the approved methods, scientific variance from approved and sanctioned methodology was considered to find nothing of value. It was reason pure and simple or inquiry had no product.

How did this ideal of science affect those committed to the scientific method? And there were dependencies on other answers in life obtainable rather than mere forays into science. Science could not direct understanding in matters of love, hate and anxiety. These were the real issues and challenges of life, with science being set outside of the common inquiries made by most people.

The effect of science's implacable influence into the lives of people to this day, complicated by sciences stepchild, technology which has grown to dominate modern life, has been given mere tacit acknowledgement.

The effect of social technology, Facebook and Twitter, has been to drive a wedge between people and their communities. Making and breaking friendships with SM is merely a click away on a computer device. Face to face socialization is more selective and more time consuming. You could get to know too much that is unacceptable through real encounters, and there is safety in pixelated and sound bite anonymity.

What is touted as socialization is isolating and misrepresents the reality about online lives.

Chapter 7

Charity

Charity has been a concern in the West for centuries. America has no designated class system as other countries do, and it has been our experience, that if there is a need, then quite often someone or some organization will step up to lend a helping hand. In a country with such wealth, there is either an inability to find the necessities of life or those in need do not know how to avail themselves of what can be found. The Bible says that the poor will always be with us, a depressing statement of fact, despite our best intentions and often ample charitable resources the extent of need is broad and deep. Even when we teach the poor to fish or giving them a fish we never seem to see the rout of hunger and need.

We are a pragmatic people, who find what needs to be done and do it, a positive attribute in the main, but the philosophical basis for much of what seems pragmatic in word and action have been influenced by a twentieth century educator and philosopher, John Dewey.

His ideas were begun to spread by he and his acolytes in the early decades of the last century. His pragmatism was sewn with what might be seen as cold and unloving details. I would not suggest that Dewey wanted the needy to remain so, but the lesson was learned by the left, in what the left would, no doubt, consider not an uncharitable understanding. Personal charity is seen as a way to condescend to the needs of others, a way to raise advantage over a lesser person.

This can be traced back further to Kant the German philosopher of the eighteenth century who held that charity and good deeds needed to be impersonal. In fact to do a good deed for sympathy or empathy was a failed deed. Dewey has given the left in America a way to give that is impersonal. It is government controlled and called welfare. We have seen how the system has been abused by welfare checks going to jailed criminals as well as deceased people.

The illegality, not to mention the shear cost that we provide to cheaters, makes the right angry and wanting to terminate the programs. This is wrong, since we have over decades continued to dismantle the legitimate charitable net under which the needy are protected from hunger and homelessness. There are more people filling for benefits, and many need help legitimately. During the Obama years the food stamp program grew by seventeen million as did fraudulent usage of the program. The faith-based system worked because you dealt with need face to face, and even though the left and Dewey, on grounds already stated, would have let the government continue to misrepresent the tax payers in this squandering of money on scammers and convicted felons, the reward for the left is a sure vote for candidates that do not rock the boat, but maintain a flawed system of theft and waste. The liberal politician will not stop abuse as it is a threat to there base, either those who vote for there own handouts or elitists who may favor a Kantian or Dewey like objection to individual charitable giving.

Chapter 8

Capitalism

Capitalism has opened doors to a comfortable life for millions of people, but financial institutions and billionaire moguls have been touted as thieves and despots. Capitalism was the only consistent objection voiced during the Wall Street sit- or sleep-in, although the context of that word, capitalism, seemed vague in meaning, or for that matter, intellectually unimportant. The gathering was unorganized, a gut movement and a loose grouping of mostly young people out of work unable to find clear articulation for their purpose. They broke a few windows and left human waste and litter everywhere. The participants soon left their confused *ad hoc* organization for new digs.

To understand why money is considered evil in the extreme, we must go back to the last century and the writings of Max Weber, a German sociologist, who coined the term "protestant ethic" and who saw the advancement of protestant countries over Catholic countries as God's not only sanction of wealth by good protestant people but a mark against the unrighteous who found only poverty and squalor. To be a Calvinist, according to Weber, was to be successful and well healed financially. The curse of wealth as it has been seen by moderns as a loose and wide-spread outgrowth of suspicion of wealthy individuals despite their country or religion. Certainly the Marxist aver that ownership is theft has driven this resentment deep into the flow of modern history. Weber and Marxism have given wealth a bad name in some circles but has not checked the pioneering and entrepreneurial spirit to the exclusion of wealth. It is unconscionable that people would purposely search out low stations in life, but the wealthy are derided for their talents or financial success. At best it is a mixed message that misrepresents one's success or failure in the world.

Banks and finance companies make tons of money, a small part of which is passed along to the client who gave them the money to invest, and then on top of the low return on investment the companies charge for investing clients' money. They are supposed to have fiduciary responsibility in handling client investment but put them in funds that they have maybe to much of. The client is not considered first. If the funds fail to do well the principle that is invested is diminished. If you are a small money-fish you get less productive funds and are charged more for the companies services. This scenario would certainly seems like misrepresentation, if it were not the procedure of countless investment companies. Historically, the banks were jealous of the financial companies having such a sweet potato and started trying to take mortgage money and invest it in the chancy markets. The Glass-Steagall Act was an attempt after the Great Depression to stop banks from investing savers' money. It was enacted in 1933 but repealed in 1999. The banking debacle of 2009 was probably due to the same banking investment policies that brought down the markets in 1929. The government passed the Dodd-Frank in 2010 which offered a token to banks "too big to fail." It has since been subject to marginal repeals of portions of the bill. The bill still allows large banks to operate an investment function, while offering frightful little help to small banks. This is a misrepresentation of banks as mortgage lenders and failed governmental aegis.

CHAPTER 9

POSSIBLE UNAVOIDABLE ORGANIZATIONS

What do you risk in being misrepresented? Even if you never formally join an organization, you are included from birth in many life structuring groups. Selective service and political party registration, Social Security and Medicare are for most Americans common groupings.

Selective service is a requirement for young men and Social Security and Medicare for most older people. Political party membership is not required but seems to chase each citizen throughout life if only by emails, mail and phone calls.

Each time one commits to membership a little bit of individual distinction is lost. The real details of membership seem to be the difficulty in belonging. You may believe in a strong country, but the government seems to embroil us in worldwide skirmishes and peacekeeping efforts. Although this may not be war, the risk to soldiers is often just as dangerous. The soldier fights to free people, but the powers that be often use the services to carryout non-militaristic goals, as if this were the normal duty of soldiers.

The Social Security Administration was originally designed to payout for a few years before death, but longer life has managed to foil that strategy and the agency is looking at fewer payers-in to provide for many longer living clients. The money will not be there to cover the many in a matter of only a few years. Likewise, Medicare was supposed to care for aging citizens for a few years until death, but our health prospects are much greater today with medical advances and again with much longer life expectancy.

These two citizen perks, Social Security and Medicare, are now political issues. People will tolerate almost any position from party candidates as long as they propose to keep these two programs and improve them for future generations. The easiest way to lose an election is to threaten these two golden calfs, but close analysis shows that these programs as they are now run will eventually bankrupt the country with no way to pay for them.

Every male eighteen years and older must sign up for the Selective Service. This seems just a mere formality, inconsequential as it stands, but, under conditions of aggression, the country may have to enlist the services of our young men and possibly young women to defend the country. Some may find war efforts behind desks or in training, but others may have to put their lives on the line for national defense.

Imagine someone drafted into a war or even volunteering, sustaining a life threatening wound which will require regular doctor visits and care. The intersection of two organizational disasters, the Sservices and Veterans' administration may complicate recovery. We cannot ignore how layers of organizational ineptitude can compound the problems of citizens depending on governmental interfacing to solve issues of health and financial support.

It is not the purpose of this book to lead you away from joining organizations but represents a caveat in choosing and trying to give direction to wandering missions and policies.

CHAPTER 10

SEEMINGLY INCONSEQUENTIAL ASSOCIATIONS

Organizational tampering is not the only compromise in beliefs and identity. Do you eat yogurt or sparrow tongues? The answer says a lot about you, a lot that you may not mean to have divulged. This is an indirect misrepresentation, but such activities can tend to create an additive undesirable effect. This effect may indicate an unofficial membership that could associate you with vegans or carnivore or freedom-hating Marxists or white-robed racist Ku Klux Klan members. Be careful of idle words and associates who use hyperbole that may be understood as definitive siding with whom you may consider undesirable.

Feminism can be represented as intersectional in that broader groupings of identification associations are brought together by overlapping commonly held identities thus making feminism less specific and more inclusive. Yet the inclusion may threaten to compromise feminists values.

Conservatives have trouble with government getting involved with daily life while bigger government is seen as a protective net for Liberals. But Libertarians believe in government staying out of the lives of citizens while favoring economic conservatism values, and getting rid of drug and prostitution laws is offensive to many Liberals and all true Conservatives is a basic Libertarian policy. Despite the presence of overlap by commonalities, Libertarians are not Republicans nor Liberals and including them is detrimental to both parties. So choosing a political party may entomb you with ideas and people you might want to avoid.

I have been a member of a neighborhood organization for decades only to realize that the leadership has selfish goals and usually not that of the general membership. Being in the directorate gives a look to electing authorities and serves self-promotion to paying government positions. Any real issue that could easily be at cross issues with the local government fathers is usually off limits. The group option involves organizing picnics, beautification of homes and aggressive clutter-removal rules which tends to keep neighborhoods under perpetual pressure to measure up and neighbor taking offense against neighbor.

I have a dear friend who is a retired college professor who over many decades of teaching has seen the weeding out of Conservative teachers and their replacement with Liberal instructors. When asked why this has happened my friend tells me it has become clear that the left does not see value in pitting opposing views. The belief is that Conservatives are wrong about their beliefs and have no seat at the table of universal ideas. The overall effect is horrible but it says more about those that hold differing opinions: they are useless in the market of ideas, useless in their life's work. Liberals see their mission as that of taking God to the mortals who are wrong by holding any other beliefs.

CONCLUSION

How do you see your identity. Is it innate, or do you see the encroachment of affiliations taking away your understanding of the world in which you live. The daily barrage of the media leaves us confused and undecided. We do not bring up what could be seen as divisive issues fearing that relationships might be compromised. What we don't say is to be in compliance with what we oppose. We probably should make a list of beliefs periodically to reinforce our identifying precepts.

Christopher Lasch, a Harvard graduate and critique of American life, eventually saw the influence of general progress as a threat to intellectual life and the commodification of all life right down to the family unit. He wrote of the failure of capitalism which had failed America. He wrote of intellectual incapacity and a fragility of self-image. Although he died several decades ago he saw the gathering storm of our time. A loss of self-image is epidemic. In stark conflict with much of what we see around us, we are trapped by acquiescence.

Clothing labels unite acolytes more than deep principles and precepts. Dress in black and you will not only very fashionable but will draw others of like camouflage. Most people want variable cover such that they are only seen through a specific chosen lens. The visual is more than fashion but a way to preview oneself. Cast yourself in the best light and hope that you can justify interest. The deeper issues are slow to emerge, if not hidden for fear of rejection. A strong to external, easily recognizable uniform can save deep discussion and the chance of going over the margins of dress.

The lack of identity is unfortunately found in soldiers returning from war. Retaining memory of loss of friends and the seeming unimportance of life. Everyday returning warriors are committing suicide. Likewise, young school children, who as Erik Ericsson claimed, are in basic developmental stages marked by bouts of inferiority and fragile personality. Commodification of youth has given an external protective uniform to help avoid wardrobe ridicule yet given also a weakness in the deeper elements of development may fate the young who are not primarily in the process of forming a sound maturity. Young people are seemingly pushed to suicide by bullies and social divisions.

The group itself is corrupted according to Gustave Le Bon's sociological mainstay *The Crowd* by luminaries and lunatic despots. One man makes the argument as the masses corrupt and rage tilting truth and missing even core understandings of the group-author's work. Original meaning is lost on the masses. The crowd does not value truth and finds opposition in those that stand against the crowd. If illusion and dishonesty are the grist of the mob's millwork, then the group must disband and recommit, as if this would be a lasting dedication to the common purpose. No, ideas are best held individually and argued together, making conversations possible. The only way that true discussion and grouping can be possible is in at least small groups, civilly and respectfully.

We have a social presence and an individual personality, an identity. When we give our blessing to an organization, then we must remember that our social presence in a group is not representative of the group 100% nor of us, and to expect, assuming and adopting the group tenets will tend to pull you away from your own personal beliefs. Belonging will levy a price for your compliance. Your insights and beliefs will be skewed in membership. Pre-determine how far you will be drawn out of your essential self and whether it is worth the loss. Avoiding all membership cannot happen except by living off the grid in a deep forest or a cave having no human contact, foraging for foods and living rough.

Epilog

To many readers, the future for joining groups may look bleak after the argument against organizations. Wrongly you may have come to believe that members are just rabble to fill out the ranks led by their noses to do the bidding of the leadership. Since it is almost impossible to avoid organizations, the future does not seem to connote a living positivity to followers.

Another way to view this realty is to see that we are all imperfect and must unite with mankind in membership heeding the caveat that their is power to be claimed, although fated power, that can unite voices and policies to a better community and a better world. Recognizing the ultimate downside for personal identity and the inefficiency of groups but dedicated to what the collective efforts may rally. Living with a sense that a failing grouping is the best for which we can hope and remaining reticent about individual and personal representation.

There is another way to see misrepresentation that also includes the imperfection of man, yet goes farther. To an orthodox Christian's belief system, however, imperfection is due to a fallen state and original sin. Traced back to Adam's fall, we see the fall and imperfection of the human race along with the rest of creation. In the beginning, all was perfect, Adam sinned and brought a curse on him and all of creation. How this version differs from the second understanding of group failure is the understanding that we can ultimately be led from imperfection and impoverishment, through faith in Jesus Christ, to an eternity in a future perfect paradise where all those who have demonstrated faith in Christ will reside forever in a group of saints who will be free of sin and misrepresentation. Christ will be our brother and we will be the perfect representation of Christ and remain with the triune God-head for all eternity.